W9-ADG-022

IN A
BACKYARD

Jen Green

CRABTREE
Publishing Company
www.crabtreebooks.com

Crabtree Publishing Company
www.crabtreebooks.com

PMB 16A, 350 Fifth Avenue
Suite 3308
New York, NY 10118

612 Welland Avenue
St. Catharines
Ontario L2M 5V6

CRABTREE:
Project editor: P. A. Finlay
Assistant editor: Carrie Gleason
Coordinating editor: Ellen Rodger

BROWN PARTWORKS:
Editor: Amanda Harman
Designer: Joan Curtis
Picture researcher: Clare Newman
Managing editor: Bridget Giles
Commissioning editor: Anne O'Daly
Consultants: J. C. Lewis, PhD
Mark Hostetler, PhD, Wildlife Specialist, University of Florida

Illustrator: Peter Bull

Photographs: Bruce Coleman Collection title page, pp 14*b*, 17,18, 23, 29; Erwin 7 Peggy Bauer/Bruce Coleman Collection front cover, p 28*m*; Jane Burton/Bruce Coleman Collection pp 4*t*, 24; John Cancalosi/Bruce Coleman Collection p 27*t*; Steven C. Kaufman/Bruce Coleman Collection p 7*t*; Dr. Scott Nielson/Bruce Coleman Collection p 30; Marie Read/Bruce Coleman Collection p 19*t*; Hans Reinhard/Bruce Coleman Collection p 8*m*; John Shaw/Bruce Coleman Collection p 6; Kim Taylor/Bruce Coleman Collection p 15; Colin Varndell/Bruce Coleman Collection p 22*t*; Ralph A. Clevenger/Corbis p 11*t*; W. Perry Conway/Corbis p 20*b*; Mark Gibson/Corbis p 25*b*; Darrell Gulin/Corbis p 22*m*; Richard Hamilton Smith/Corbis front cover, back cover, p 5; George Lepp/Corbis p 11*b*, 25*t*; Buddy Mays/Corbis p 10; Joe McDonald/Corbis pp 13, 19*b*, 27*b*; Mary Ann McDonald/Corbis p 16*t*; Michael Pole/Corbis p 31; Lynda Richardson/Corbis p 16*m*; Michael Melford Inc/Image Bank p 3; G. I. Bernard/NHPA p 14*t*; Robert Erwin/NHPA p 20*t*; T. Kitchin & V. Hurst p 4*m*, 26; Rich Kirchner/NHPA p 7*b*; Rod Planck/NHPA p 9; John Shaw/NHPA p 8*t*; Karl Switak/NHPA p 28*b*

Created and produced by
Brown Partworks Limited

First edition
10 9 8 7 6 5 4 3 2 1
Copyright © 2002 Brown Partworks Limited
Printed in Singapore

CATALOGING-IN-PUBLICATION DATA

Green, Jen.
    In a backyard / Jen Green.
      p. cm. -- (Small worlds)
    Contents: Backyards of the world -- Life in the backyard -- Creepers and crawlers -- Flying visitors -- The great and small -- What is in your backyard?
    Summary: Describes the various animals that live in and around the backyard and garden of a house in North America.
      ISBN 0-7787-0141-7 (RHC) -- ISBN 0-7787-0155-7 (pbk.)
    1. Urban animals--Juvenile literature. [1. Urban animals. 2. Animals.] I. Small worlds (New York, N.Y.).
    QL49 .G74 2002
    591.75'6--dc21

2001047296
LC

Contents

Backyards of the world

You do not need to visit a zoo or the countryside to see wild animals. Hundreds of animals live right in your own backyard!

▲ *Not all the animals you see in your backyard are wild. This pet cat is on the lookout for small birds and mammals, such as shrews or mice, to chase.*

▶ *Coyotes are doglike animals common in most of North America. This one has entered a backyard and is sniffing around the door of the house.*

▶ *Some animals prefer big, overgrown gardens. Others like tiny areas in crowded cities. Whatever its size, your backyard is a small world with wildlife.*

Backyards around the world are home to many different kinds of animals, including mammals, birds, insects, reptiles, and amphibians. Some backyard animals are big, but most are small, so you have to look carefully to find them. This book will introduce you to some of the species, or types of animals, that live in backyards and gardens throughout North America.

Life in the Backyard

falcon

mockingbird

opossum

crow

bat

hummingbird

songbirds

house cat

mouse

All animals need food, water, and shelter. Your backyard provides all of these, making it a great place for many animals.

Different types of animals live in different areas of your backyard. Worms, ants, and moles live under the lawn. Centipedes, snails, and sow bugs lurk under stones and in damp corners. Woodpiles may attract snakes and lizards. Toads, frogs, and newts visit garden ponds. Wasps, bats, and spiders prefer to live in backyard sheds.

dragonfly

pond turtle

Creepers and crawlers
Even small back-yards are home to thousands of insects, spiders, and other small animals.

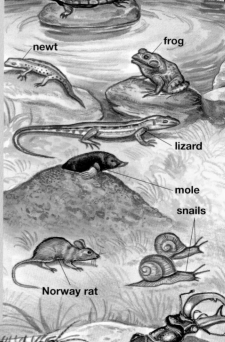

newt

frog

lizard

mole

snails

Norway rat

slug

centipede

worm

stag beetle

earwig

sow bug

ants

rattlesnake

chipmunk

squirrel

downy
woodpecker

fox

raccoon

field rat

monarch
butterfly

robin

skunk

baby robins

Animals big and small

Squirrels are tree-dwelling mammals that are active in the daytime. Larger mammals, such as deer and foxes, might visit the yard at night.

monarch
butterfly

Flying visitors

Birds visit your backyard to hunt worms, slugs, and insects, or to peck at seeds and bread crumbs you have left out for them.

rabbit

bee

monarch
butterfly
caterpillar

ladybug

garden
spider

aphid

Creepers and crawlers

Insects are the most common animals in your backyard. Some are a nuisance, while others are helpful to gardeners.

▲ *The hover fly looks like a bee or a wasp. Hover flies get their name because they hover over flowers before climbing in to collect nectar.*

▶ *Fast and agile, dragonflies are acrobats of the air. Their two pairs of wings do not work as one unit but flap as pairs.*

The creepy crawlers in your garden include many insects, such as ants, earwigs, beetles, dragonflies, and butterflies. Insects eat all kinds of foods, including plants and other insects. Some beetle grubs dig into logs and tree trunks to eat wood. Other insects eat dung or the remains of dead animals.

▶ *Monarch butterflies enter backyards in the fall during their lengthy **migrations** south and in the summer as they fly north again.*

The beauties and the pests

Beetles are the largest group of insects. They include ladybugs, June beetles, weevils, and large stag beetles with mouthparts that look like deer antlers. In spring, male stag beetles wrestle with each other for the chance to mate with a female. If your backyard has a pond in it or a stream nearby, dragonflies might be around. These large insects are fierce **predators** that hunt other insects while flying.

Butterflies are some of the most beautiful insects that visit your yard. The colorful markings on their wings are formed by thousands of tiny scales. Many of these insects feed on flower nectar, which they suck using their long, strawlike mouthparts. They flutter around colorful shrubs and flowers, such as lantana and daisies.

Insects such as aphids and black flies are gardeners' least favorite visitors. Aphids suck the sap from plants.

▼ *Male stag beetles use their large antler-like mouthparts to fight other males.*

They can cause a lot of damage to some flowers, such as roses. In warm weather, these pests breed very quickly and can infest entire neighborhoods.

Insect homes

Most types of insects do not live together in large numbers, but all ants and some bees and wasps live in groups called colonies. In early summer, you may discover an ants' nest in the backyard. The nest contains at least one large female ant, called the queen, who spends her time laying eggs. All the other ants are her children. They are mostly female workers, who look after and feed the young ants and the queen. They also clean, guard the nest, and search for food outside.

A beehive works in a similar way to an ant colony. It has a queen bee, a few males called drones, and thousands of female workers.

▲ *Ladybugs feed on sap-sucking aphids. These red and black beetles help keep the number of pesky aphids down.*

▼ *These worker ants are carrying a young developing ant to a safer place in their nest.*

FANTASTIC FACTS

● Aphids release a sweet liquid called honeydew after sucking sap from plants.

● Ants love sweet foods. They "milk" aphids for honeydew and sometimes collect the aphids to keep near their nest.

The worker bees collect nectar from flowers and bring it back to the nest to make honey. They also collect pollen to eat. As the bees fly from plant to plant, they carry pollen from one flower to another, helping the plants make their seeds. In this way, bees help your garden grow.

Cycle of life

Bees, beetles, ants, and butterflies have four-stage life cycles. From eggs, they hatch into caterpillars or legless grubs such as maggots. These **larvae** feed and grow and become **pupae**, after which they emerge as adults. The change from larva to adult is called metamorphosis. Butterfly pupae grow into adults inside hard coverings called chrysalises.

▶ *This diagram shows the egg, caterpillar, chrysalis, and adult stages of a monarch butterfly.*

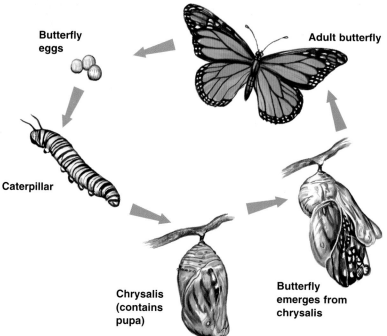

Butterfly eggs

Adult butterfly

Caterpillar

Chrysalis (contains pupa)

Butterfly emerges from chrysalis

The backyard at night

Many backyard animals cannot be seen during the day. Snails, sow bugs, centipedes, and many other species are mostly **nocturnal**, or active at night. Moths, such as the white line sphinx moth shown below, are night flyers.

Night flyers are attracted to light and flutter around windows. Fireflies flash their little lights, making the yard look magical. Flashing is the way that fireflies speak to each other and attract mates.

You will see more insects in your garden in the summer than in the winter. Queen wasps, ladybugs, and butterflies live in sheds and woodpiles in the winter, but the cold kills most insects. Although many of the adults do not make it, their eggs and pupae survive in the soil and hatch the next spring.

Although they resemble beetles, sow bugs are not insects. They are related to water-living crabs, shrimp, and lobsters.

Damp hideaways and venomous hunters

Sow bugs, centipedes, and millipedes like damp, dark places in the backyard. They hide under stones during the day and look for food at night. Centipedes are predators. They hunt small insects on their many legs and stab prey with their fangs. Sow bugs and millipedes are slow moving herbivores that feed on rotting plants.

Spiders belong to the group of animals called arachnids. Arachnids also include scorpions.

Banded garden spiders live in parks and yards across most of North America. They catch flying insects in their sticky webs, which they spin in bushes and shrubs.

14

Spiders hunt insects and other spiders for food. Many spiders catch their prey by weaving webs of sticky thread. Most spiders paralyze their prey by injecting poison, or **venom**, with their fangs. Some spider venom is strong enough to make a person very sick. Luckily, these spiders do not usually live in our backyards!

Slugs, snails, and worms

Slugs and snails are invertebrates, or animals without a spine, and they have soft, slimy bodies. Snails have a hard shell for protection, but slugs have only a small shell inside their body or no shell at all. They move along on their wide, flat bellies, leaving a slimy trail behind. At night, slugs and snails nibble garden plants, especially areas of new growth. Most gardeners see slugs and snails as pests.

Earthworms are long, thin, legless animals that live underground. A large yard can contain thousands of worms! Worms tunnel through the earth by swallowing soil and digesting the plant and animal matter it contains. The waste soil passes through the worm's body and is pushed up to the ground's surface, leaving a wormcast on the lawn. Unlike most slugs and snails, earthworms are very good for the garden.

▲ Snails rest during the day. They gather in dark, damp places, out of the drying sun.

▼ Worms help mix the soil and allow air and water to reach the lower layers. Worms improve the soil for growing plants, which makes gardeners happy.

Flying visitors

Birds are among the most colorful animals to visit your backyard. At dusk, you can also see fluttering bats, as they hunt moths and other insects flying in the darkening sky.

▲ *This woodpecker pecks at the tree bark for insects. It grips the tree trunk tightly with its clawed feet.*

▶ *Flocks of starlings gather in backyards to feed on seeds, worms, insects, and snails.*

There are more than 9,000 different species of birds in the world. To help study them, scientists divide birds into 27 different groups, called orders. The largest order is the songbirds, with more than 5,000 species. Songbirds include most of the birds that visit your backyard, such as crows, starlings, thrushes, chickadees, and finches.

▶ *Blue jays, such as this baby, are among the noisiest backyard birds. They are found in yards, parks, and woodlands in eastern North America.*

Northern mockingbirds are the state bird of five U.S. states.

Garden bird song

Songbirds are also known as perching birds. Their feet have three toes facing forward and one facing backward. This arrangement helps the birds lock their feet securely around branches, so they do not fall off when resting at night.

The beautiful sounds of bird songs can be heard in most backyards, even in big cities. Their chorus is loud in the evening and even louder at dawn, when the birds wake up. Mockingbirds are songbirds that mimic the calls of other birds and can be heard in backyards across North America.

FANTASTIC FACTS

● Songbirds sing to let other birds know they are in the area.

● Male mockingbirds sing all day and sometimes at night.

● Different songbirds have different songs, so birds of a species can recognize each other.

Flocking together

House sparrows and starlings are common in city gardens. These birds originally lived only in Europe, Africa, and Asia. Now they are widespread in North America, too. House sparrows and starlings live in flocks, which helps protect them from danger. As the flock feeds, the birds take turns to check for predators. If one bird spies a hawk, the whole group takes off together.

Color in the garden

Cardinals, bluebirds, and robins are among the most colorful songbirds in your garden. Like many bird species, the females are less colorful than the males. For example, female eastern bluebirds are very dull in color, but males have a bright blue back and a red chest. The males are bright to attract and impress the females. The females need dull colors to hide on the nest.

Hummingbirds are small, dainty birds that brighten backyard gardens during the spring and summer months. They are named for the humming sounds their wings make as they flutter up and down at great speed. Their flapping wings help the birds stay still in the air. Hummingbirds build tiny, cup-shaped nests in which to lay their eggs.

▲ *This northern cardinal is easily identified as a male because it is bright red. The female cardinal is brown.*

◄ *Hummingbirds use their flying skills to hover around flowers. Their long bill helps them reach the sweet nectar inside.*

Nesting times

Throughout the seasons, birds follow a breeding cycle, which you can see in your own backyard. As the weather warms in spring, the birds sing loudly to find mates and set up breeding areas. Then they pair up, build their nests, and lay their eggs. When the eggs hatch, parent birds bring food to the nestlings, or baby birds. In the summer, you can see young birds hopping after their parents on the lawn or practicing their flying skills.

▼ *Like crows, magpies often raid other birds' nests and steal their eggs.*

Other bird visitors

Blue jays, magpies, and crows are all members of the same family. These intelligent, adaptable birds feed on a wide range of foods, including insects, reptiles, frogs, and small mammals. Some bird species in your backyard live there all year. Others visit only at certain times of the year. Different species may drop in to your yard as they fly north or south on long migrations.

In the spring, swallows arrive to nest and raise their chicks in North America. In the fall, some species of swallows fly south to South America to spend the winter in a warmer place.

Flying mammals

Flying bats can also be found in some backyards. Unlike birds, bats have no feathers. Their wings are covered by skin instead. Bats are nocturnal and spend the daylight hours asleep in sheds, hollow trees, or attics. They leave their **roost** at night to hunt for food.

Bats cannot see very well at night, but they have excellent hearing. They track their insect prey using echolocation. As the bat flies through the air, it produces high-pitched clicking sounds. The sound waves from these clicks spread out and bounce off objects such as flying insects. The bat listens for the returning echoes, targets its prey, and swoops in for the kill. The echoes also help the bat steer a safe course through the air, around obstacles such as trees.

FANTASTIC FACTS

● Bats are big eaters. Some can eat as many as 3,500 flying insects in just one night!

● Bats have a lot of food available to them. Most insect-eating birds fly and hunt during the day, leaving more prey for the bats at night.

▼ *This bat is using echolocation to catch a moth in midair.*

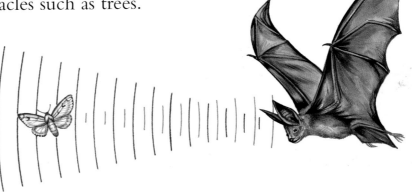

The big and the small

Frogs, lizards, and snakes are part of the miniature zoo in some backyards. Mammals, such as squirrels and foxes, also visit.

▲ *Rats live close to areas where there is plenty of garbage and other scraps to feed on.*

▶ *With dark face markings like masks, raccoons look like bandits. Their clawed paws make them excellent grabbers and good climbers.*

Biologists divide the animal kingdom into two main groups: vertebrates and invertebrates. Vertebrates are animals with a bony skeleton inside their body. Invertebrates do not have an inner skeleton. Your yard is home to many invertebrates, including insects, worms, snails, and spiders.

▶ *These baby squirrels depend on their mother to look after them. They will be able to leave the nest when they are about seven weeks old.*

Vertebrates, such as mammals, birds, reptiles, and amphibians, also live there. Mammals are the group of furry animals whose young feed on their mother's milk. Bats make up about one-quarter of all mammal species. Rodents are the biggest mammal group, containing nearly half of all mammal species. This group includes squirrels, chipmunks, rats, and mice.

Nibblers and gnawers

All rodents have strong teeth called incisors. They are used for biting and gnawing. Mice and squirrels are mainly plant eaters, gnawing on nuts, seeds, and buds. They sometimes damage garden plants. Rats are omnivores, eating both vegetables and the flesh of dead animals.

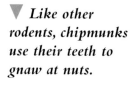

▼ *Like other rodents, chipmunks use their teeth to gnaw at nuts.*

Pocket gophers are named for the fur-lined food pockets in their cheeks. These burrowing animals are common in the southwestern U.S.

Rodents live in different places in the backyard. Squirrels live in the treetops. Rats and mice find shelter in sheds. Gophers are burrowing mammals that live underground.

Squirrels and chipmunks are different from other backyard mammals, because they are **diurnal**, or active during the day. You can see them sitting upright on a tree stump, nibbling at a nut held in their paws. Mice come out at night. They are small and nocturnal so we rarely see them in our gardens and backyards.

Unpopular guests

Moles live in most regions of North America. They are among the least popular animals that move into our backyards. Many gardeners do not like the mole's tunneling activities because they leave mounds called molehills on the lawn, wrecking the smooth, grassy surface. A mole's body is built for burrowing. This small animal has strong front paws and long claws, which dig and shovel the earth at the same time.

With their strong claws, moles are expert tunnelers. They have poor eyesight, and rely on their sensitive nose to find tasty earthworms to eat.

FANTASTIC FACTS

● Virginia opossums are the only marsupials that live in North America.

● Marsupials are a group of mammals whose young, after being born, finish developing in a pouch on their mother's stomach.

▼ *People are sometimes forced to burn clothes that have been sprayed by skunks, because the smell is so bad!*

People sometimes see raccoons, foxes, and opossums in their garden, even in the center of crowded cities. At night, these visitors sometimes rummage through the garbage for scraps of food to eat.

Forest mammals

If there are woods near your home, your yard might be visited by deer, skunks, and other forest animals. Deer are large mammals, but their brown or spotted coats provide such good **camouflage** that these shy, beautiful animals are seldom seen. Skunks are a little more obvious, with their black and white stripes. People move carefully around skunks, because of their well-known ability to squirt a foul-smelling spray at intruders.

Reptiles

Snakes, lizards, turtles, crocodiles, and alligators are all examples of reptiles. Most of these scaly-skinned animals breed by laying eggs. Lizards are generally small reptiles, most common in warm areas, such as the southern United States and Mexico.

You can see lizards sunning themselves on rocks, on garden walls, or darting across the yard chasing insects. Watch for the males to expand a brightly colored patch of skin under their head, called a dewlap. They often do little pushups at the same time. Together, these behaviors warn other lizards to stay away from the performer's **territory** or their mates.

Turtles and lizards are usually welcome in our yards, but snakes are usually discouraged. Many people are frightened of snakes because some are venomous. However, most snakes do not harm humans. Some people like snakes, because they eat pests such as mice and rats. Some species, such as the scarlet king snake, even feed on venomous snakes!

▲ *Collared lizards are brightly colored reptiles. They feed on other lizards and insects. This one has caught a big beetle.*

▼ *Turtles, such as this eastern box turtle, visit yards in wooded areas near streams and rivers.*

Dangerous snakes

Some regions in North America are home to venomous snakes, including cottonmouths, coral snakes, copperheads, and rattlesnakes.

Rattlesnakes are named for the "rattle" of loose scales on their tail, which they shake to frighten intruders away. Rattlesnakes are also known as pit vipers because of the heat-sensitive pits on their heads. The snakes use their heat sensors to track warm-blooded prey, such as rabbits and mice, even in the dark, late at night.

▼ *Tiger salamanders are the largest salamanders that live on land.*

Amphibians

Frogs, toads, newts, and salamanders are amphibians. Amphibians are animals that live in water and on land. Some amphibians spend their whole life in streams and ponds. Others live on land but return to the water during the breeding season.

Frogs are predators that shoot out their long, sticky tongue to capture passing insects.

In spring, you can hear the loud, croaking sounds frogs make to attract mates. Frogs and toads are related animals. We usually give those species with smooth, moist skin the common name "frog," while we usually give the name "toad" to those with dry and warty skin.

Like insects, amphibians have life cycles. Frogs lay their gel-covered eggs in ponds and streams. The eggs hatch into plump, legless tadpoles, which swim by wriggling their long tail. After about eight weeks, the tadpole sprouts back legs, then front legs. The tadpole's tail shrinks as it slowly changes into an adult frog.

FANTASTIC FACTS

● Many frogs have pouches in their throat that they fill with air to make their calls even louder during the mating season.

● The female American bullfrog can lay as many as 10,000 eggs at a time.

◄ If you have a pond in your backyard, it might be visited by a toad. These amphibians like to live under leaves and logs near water. They feed on worms, insects, and other invertebrates.

What is in your backyard?

The smallest backyard can be a retreat for wildlife. Welcome birds and insects by putting out food and growing their favorite plants.

▲ *A good way to feed birds is to hang freshly cut fruit, such as apples and oranges, from a tree or shrub in your backyard.*

To attract birds to your yard, put food on a hanging bird table. The birds can feed safely there, away from cats and other garden predators. Ask an adult to help you make the table, with a wooden board about twelve inches long and eight inches wide (30 cm long and 20 cm wide). Make a container for the seed by gluing narrow strips of wood around the board's edge. To prevent the seed from rotting, be sure the bottom of the table has tiny holes in it so that water can drain away. Line the bottom of the table with wire mesh that is too small for the seed to fall out but lets water pass through. Screw a hook into each side of the board, then attach string to the hooks. Hang the table from a tree branch.

Birds will eat all kinds of kitchen scraps, including bread, cheese, and bacon rind.

▶ *If you keep quiet and very still, you can sometimes get up very close to the wildlife in your yard.*

Do not leave these treats out in early summer, when they can choke nestlings. To attract hummingbirds to your garden, use a feeder (you can buy one from a pet store). Buy a notebook to record all the species you see at the bird table. Which foods are most popular with which birds?

Grow sweet-smelling plants to attract moths and butterflies to your backyard. Moths will visit if you plant honeysuckle, which smells strongly at night. Butterflies flock around verbena and wallflowers. Ask your parents if you can plant a buddleia, or butterfly bush.

TOP TIPS FOR ANIMAL WATCHERS

1 Binoculars can help you study animals at a distance. A magnifying glass will help you see small animals close up.

2 Most of the animals in your yard are easily scared off. Keep as still and quiet as possible. Get behind a bush to watch mammals and birds.

3 You will need a shaded flashlight to study nocturnal animals. Stick a piece of red cellophane over the glass of your flashlight to give it a red glow.

Words to know

camouflage Colors and patterns that help an animal blend in with its surroundings.

diurnal Describes an animal that sleeps at night and is active during the day.

migration A journey made by animals to escape cold weather, find food, or reach a safe place to breed.

nocturnal Describes an animal that sleeps during the day and is active at night.

predator An animal that hunts other animals for food.

pupa The life stage between the larva and the adult, when an insect rebuilds its body.

roost A place where flying animals such as birds and bats rest at night.

territory A breeding or feeding area that an animal defends against other animals.

venom Poison that is injected. Many snakes are venomous.

Index